31 Days of Affirmations to Guide You to

Glow up, sis
Glow up

Courtney Arlesia

Limits of Liability and Disclaimer of Warranty

The author and publisher shall not be liable for your misuse of this material. This book is strictly for informational and educational purposes. The purpose of this book is to educate and entertain. The author and/or publisher do not guarantee that anyone following these techniques, suggestions, tips, ideas, or strategies will become successful. The author and/or publisher shall have neither liability nor responsibility to anyone with respect to any loss or damage caused, or alleged to be caused, directly or indirectly by the information contained in this book.

Views expressed in this publication do not necessarily reflect the views of the publisher.

COVER Lyric Abbott of Visionary Palette

Printed in the United States of America

ISBN 978-1-948270-19-9
Keen Vision Publishing, LLC
www.keen-vision.com

Cindy,

Thank you for your love & support.

May you continue to glow into the woman God has called you to be!

With love,

CA

Glow up, Sis!

Hey Sis,

If you are reading this, you are in the right place. It's time to glow to your highest potential. No, I'm not talking about the temporary glow you get after a good facial. This glow up starts from the inside and radiates into every environment, situation, obstacle, circumstance, victory, or failure you may encounter. My name is Courtney Clardy, but many call me Courtney Arlesia. Although I have never met you, I'm sure our daily stories and struggles are similar. That makes us closer than most would like to admit. I put together this book of affirmations just for us. Yes, US!

One day, I was sitting in my room thinking. I wanted an affirmation book that would be perfect for me; one that was filled with positivity, yet real. I desired a book of affirmations that would meet me where I was and give me that, "Girl, get yourself together!" moment when I needed it. That's what sisters do, right? We make sure we get it together! After searching high and low for that book, I finally decided to write it myself.

One of my favorite sayings is, "In order for us to glow up, we must first grow up." As you read this book, imagine that we are talking on the phone, and I am affirming your glow up while holding you accountable to becoming the best you. I truly believe that we must encourage ourselves. However, we also need people in our circle who will uplift and pour into us. Well, sis, HERE I AM. I am in your circle and ready to encourage you each day you flip a page in this book. Remember, glowing up doesn't happen overnight. It is a process we must commit to daily. I hope these 31 days of affirmations from me to you will push you to be the best you.

With love,

Courtney Arlesia

DAY ONE

I'm Great!

You are the epitome of greatness. Say to yourself today, "Forget what haters say, I'M GREAT." No one can stop your greatness. You are great today and every day going forward.

We often encounter people who do their best to remind us of our shortcomings, failures, and flaws. People will speak to our past before they pour into our present and speak life into our future. Can we be honest for a minute? Sometimes, those people are the ones who are close to us. They can even be family and so-called friends. In order for us to reach our full glow, we must drown out negativity and let the haters hate. We must continue to glow up in spite of. There is a saying that suggests we let the hate of others motivate us. I say, view hate as if it were water: Let it roll off your back! We don't need hate to motivate us. We have enough motivation without having to work so hard to prove our greatness. The truth is, people will always have something to say. It doesn't matter if we are doing bad or good. Our job isn't to change people's minds about us. Instead, our job is to make sure we are always walking in our purpose. Sis, make the declaration of greatness over your life and don't allow anyone to take that greatness from you.

DAY TWO

Hustle

Everything you desire is in your hustle. Pray for it, pray over it, then get up and GO GET IT!

isten, faith without works is dead. That's scripture! (See James 2:17.) Praying without making moves will get you NOWHERE. In order for God to do what He has already planned, you must trust Him enough to make the first step and put some hustle behind it. The business He has ordained for you is not going to come and knock on your door. The book He has instructed you to write will not write itself. The agency He desires to position you in will not call you back if you don't go to the audition. You must get up and chase each of your dreams and God-given desires.

Also, be sure you are doing everything in your power to perfect your craft. You may be an amazing singer, but that doesn't mean you don't need voice lessons. Voice lessons are vital to making sure your beautiful voice gets better and stronger with time. No matter what your craft is, vow to get better at it. Don't set yourself up for failure. Get on your hustle daily.

This is only the beginning. Every day is a new day to get better. Use this day to improve!

The beauty in seeing a new sunrise is knowing that it presents another opportunity to get better. Some days, we wake up and complain about going to work. At times, we don't even want to get out of bed. Sis, we must realize that with every complaint, we play ourselves. So, get up! Get up with a heart of gratitude, set your intentions for the day, and get better. Maybe yesterday wasn't the best day for you. So, what? Acknowledge it, but do not dwell in it. Why not dwell? Because you have been presented with the opportunity to do it over and do it better. Let yesterday remain in the past. Focus on all the greatness that you can do in your future. Declare that today will be better, believe that today will be better, and walk in your better today.

DAY FOUR

The Process

You won't get to the place you desire to be in life instantly. It is a process. You'll get there, sis. Just take it one day at a time.

Have you ever seen a plant grow immediately after a seed is placed in the soil? I surely haven't. The plant must endure a process underground before we see its growth on the surface. This process doesn't happen overnight. Much like a plant, our process to glow up won't happen overnight either. Instead of rushing our process and attempting to skip steps, we must appreciate every high and low we endure in the process. Endurance builds character. Character molds and shapes us for the rest of our lives. Instant gratification doesn't last forever, sis. If we settle for instant, we will always be in search of more. Live one day at a time and take advantage of every learning opportunity that presents itself. That's how we get better. That's how we truly build. Embrace your process. Don't run from it.

DAY FIVE

Positive
vibes Only

Today, do something positive that will push you
closer to your goals.

Get out of bed. Get off your bottom. Make a list of the goals you desire and need to accomplish today. Make sure your goals are attainable and do not put too much pressure on yourself. Don't forget to list steps on how you will reach each goal. Make sure that every goal is a positive one. Yes, Sis, it is possible to make negative goals. Pray for clarity about what needs to be done and how you can get there. You may have a goal as simple as: Make everyday a good day. The steps you can take to meet that goal would be: smile often, give compliments, walk away from negativity because you know it doesn't serve you, and speak positive affirmations over yourself. The only way you will meet your goals is by taking the steps to do so.

DAY SIX

Celebrate

Listen, sis. Pity parties are no fun. Get up and throw yourself a party that's worth having. Maybe you are not where you want to be, but you are not in the same place you were yesterday.... that's worth celebrating.

It's hard to celebrate yourself when you are not meeting your goals or if you are not in the place you envisioned. However, if you don't celebrate you, then who will? Don't expect others to throw a party full of life for you when the party you throw for yourself is full of bitterness and sadness. Trust me, despite how you feel you, you still have something to celebrate. Let me share a truth with you, sis. I lost my first child through a second trimester miscarriage. I was 18 weeks and 7 days pregnant, so I had the same labor experience as a woman who had a full-term pregnancy. Somedays are good and somedays are not so good, but I promised myself to celebrate my child and myself.

Life will happen to us. At times, it will cause us to feel stuck. We may even feel like there is no reason to fight for tomorrow. I'm here to tell you that if you wake up to see another sunrise: You have a reason to celebrate! Don't focus on your losses or what you don't have yet. Every step to healing, meeting your goals, obtaining your degree, writing that song, and starting the business is worth celebrating. If you take one step to meet your goal, no matter how big or small it is, you must celebrate it!

DAY SEVEN

Be You

You are talented, authentic, and unique. No one is like you. They may have similarities, but they could never, ever be you. Stay true to who you are, sis. The world only has access to one of you. Don't let us down by attempting to be someone else.

We are living in an age where it feels like everyone is doing the same thing. We are constantly comparing ourselves and, at times, even doubting ourselves. Everyone is talented and possesses a gift, but no one is you, sis! What God gave you is unique and the world needs it. When God created you, He had a specific design in mind. You may look like your mother and father, or even your Great Aunt Helen, but God placed something inside of you unlike anything He placed in any other creation. Instead of seeing how you can be more like the woman on the cover of Ebony magazine, spend time tapping into being more like the woman you were created to be. After all, being like someone else will eventually become boring and unsatisfying. The true joy you seek is found in your ability and freedom to be your unique self.

Don't put yourself in a box of comparison. Step outside of the box and operate in your gift. What you have may not be for everybody, but it is for somebody. Focus on you, your gift, and how you can give it to the world daily.

DAY EIGHT

Purpose

You will be in the presence of people who will give your gift purpose and through that, you can walk in your purpose.

Come on sis, say it with me, "I will be in the presence of people who will give my gift purpose and through that, I can walk in my purpose." Say it over and over until you truly believe that your gift will make room for you. We can become so focused on what the room should look like that we miss the most important piece: Our gift is wherever we are. When we are at the store, walking down the street, or even clocking in at work, our gift is with us. Therefore, we must choose to walk in it. Let's say you are rushing in the convenient store to get coffee. On the way in, you hold the door open for someone with a huge smile on your face. That person thanks you, and tells you that you have made their day. You have just walked in your gift! Yes, it can be that simple! God strategically places us in the presence of others to give our gift purpose. Remember, your gift isn't just how creative and talented you are. Your gift is also your smile, your extreme amount of patience, your contagious and loving personality, and your corny jokes that make people laugh. Share your gift and walk in your purpose – always.

DAY NINE

Go Forward!

Are you still holding onto the past? Be honest with yourself. Now is the time to let the past go. It no longer serves you. Learn from it and keep pushing forward.

The past does not serve you. If you are wondering why they hurt you, why they lied, or even why you made the countless mistakes, it's because it was necessary. I don't know anyone who has a perfect life. Instead of wallowing in the pain, search for the lesson in it, then move forward. Those are the only two reasons you should be addressing your past. It's done now, and you cannot change a thing.

God still loves you no matter what happened. You are still His child. Nothing in your past can stop you from receiving the blessings God has in store for you! Well, I take that back. There is one person who might delay your blessings: YOU. When we make the decision to allow our past to weigh us down, we overlook the path in front of us. God cannot give us anything new when we will not let go of the old. Open yourself up to the endless possibilities and blessings that God has for you. Forgive those who hurt you and forgive yourself for hurting others.

Finally, restore your trust in God. Sometimes, things happen and we can't understand why God allowed it. In these instances, we become angry and refuse to let go. Understand that God knows and He understands. Trust Him with the pain of your past and allow Him to lead you to a path of healing.

DAY TEN

Check You!

Listen, sis. It's not always everyone else. Sometimes, it is you. Check yourself, check your attitude, and check your energy.

It's easy to point the finger and blame everyone else. However, the problem may be the person playing the blame game. No one is perfect, sis – not even you! When you think people are doing you wrong, you must take a step back and evaluate your attitude. Don't get me wrong, I know people will make you want to pull your hair out of your head, but everyone doesn't deserve your energy. Life will bring good times and bad times, but how is your attitude at all times? I'm not saying fake like you're happy and unbothered when situations upset you. However, you must learn how to handle all situations in a way that is healthy for yourself and others. A negative attitude, a smart mouth, and bad energy hurts you more than it hurts anyone else. What is bothering you today? Have you prayed about it? Is it worth addressing? If it's worth addressing, how can you address it with positivity on your end? If it's not worth addressing, then move on and be open to the goodness that the day holds for you. Every day holds beautiful goodness! Don't overlook it because of the negativity that may come your way. Remember to always be aware of the energy you are putting in the atmosphere. Check yourself often and remember that you are only responsible for how you react to others, not how others respond to you.

DAY ELEVEN

Friends

Friends come and friends go, but before you go and get rid of friends, ask yourself if you have been a good friend. To have good friends, you must first be one. Check on a friend today. See if they need something. Tell them you love them.

There once was a time when I would cut people off quickly and efficiently. One day, I grew up and realized that some people are truly worth fighting for. I don't know any relationship that is perfect, but I know plenty that I'm not letting go of. I had to stop and ask myself, "Courtney, are you a good friend? Are you giving, kind, and loving? Or, are you loving with limits, not truly trusting, and not allowing true foundations to be built?" I realized that it was the latter for most of my friendships. Listen, hurt runs deep, but everyone is not out to hurt you. Build your friendships and most importantly, pour into them. Bless your friends as much as they bless you. Learn their love language and love on them. Show your friends, your village, and your team how important they are to you. Let them know you value them. Honor is one of the highest forms of love. Don't just honor your parents and your mate! Honor those who have been down with you and plan on staying down. Call your bestie today or make the steps to mend a broken friendship. If you don't know what to say, start by saying, "I know it's been awhile and before we hash it out, just know that I love you and value our friendship. Can we work it out?" After that, allow God to do the rest!

DAY TWELVE
No Stress

Somethings are out of your control. Don't stress yourself over it. Do what you can do, wash your hands with it, and let God handle the rest.

I know that letting go is easier said than done. I know that relinquishing control is harder than people attempt to make it sound. However, learning when to hold on and when to let go is the best thing you can do for yourself. Situations will happen that are beyond our control. There will be absolutely nothing we can do to stop or fix them. Instead of stressing out, accept it. I honestly dislike the phrase, "It is what it is," but sometimes, "IT IS WHAT IT IS!" Stressing doesn't make it better. Being overly anxious and worried won't change a thing. Take a deep breath, pray about it, and give it up to the Most High. No, the situation may not work out in an instant, but God works miracles daily. I'm sure that whatever you are stressing over, God has already worked out. He is just waiting on you to let Him handle it. So, what are you waiting on, sis? Let HIM handle it.

DAY THIRTEEN

Chunk the Deuces

If it is not serving you, LET IT GO. Be okay with letting it go. You cannot get to where you need to go holding on to people, places, and things that drain you and take away from you. Chunk them deuces up and brush your shoulders off.

We will hold on for dear life to people, places, things, and situations that are draining us. Why? What are we afraid we will lose if we let go? It can't be peace because it's already missing from the equation. If it brings more tears than laughter, if you are constantly stressed and confused, if you feel weighed down, or if you find yourself trying to prove to other people why it's working when deep down inside you know that it is not; it's time to let it go. I used to think that I could get to where I'm supposed to go and take everybody with me, but the truth is everybody is not meant to go. You want to travel the world but you are stuck at a dead in job, let it go. You are chasing your dreams and your significant other has more negative things to say than positive, let it go. You drink all the time 24/7, you say it's recreational but it's getting out of hand and isn't good for your health. Let it go. God never removes without replacing. He will take whatever is holding you back and replace it with what you need to help you move forward. Chunk up your deuces!

DAY FOURTEEN
Stay Lit

If you woke up this morning, you are not only blessed but you are LIT! Let your light shine for the world to see.

If you haven't heard *Blessed* by Fred Hammond, now is the time to pull out your Apple Music, Spotify, Tidal, or whatever you use to stream music, find this song, and blast it as loud as you can! As the old folks say, "Somebody didn't get to see this morning," but you did. Get up and be grateful for it. Despite the day you may be having, if you reflect on the many blessings you have, you'll have a reason to get up and dance. You are blessed! You are lit! You are GLOWING!

DAY FIFTEEN

It Is Well

You've done well, you are doing well, and every day you will get better.

It may not look like it, it may not even feel like it, but, Sis, you are doing more than well. You have come so far from the place you were in yesterday. You have triumphed over situations that should have knocked you out and left you breathless. You have overcome adversity after adversity. Stop looking at what you don't have and stop comparing yourself to those around you. Keep getting better. Your glow up isn't based on what everyone else is doing. Your glow up is based on your will, your want, and your drive. Earlier in our journey, I said there would be no pity parties – that's what I meant. Celebrate every accomplishment thus far, speak kind words over yourself, and keep pushing forward. You've got this!

DAY SIXTEEN
Silence

Every move you make in your life doesn't have to be a post on social media. Move in silence sis. You have nothing to prove to anyone else. Just take a break from your phone today.

When did we become so obsessed with telling Facebook, Twitter, Instagram, Snapchat, and other social media sites our every move? What are we trying to prove? Do we get some sort of gratification from it? I've gotten to the point where I write a status and right before I post it, I ask myself, "What is your purpose for posting this?" Everyone does not need to know that my Double Chocolate Chip Frappuccino from Starbucks just gave me life. Don't get me wrong: I'm not judging. However, we give too much of ourselves to a lot of people and that is draining. Monitor what you post and your purpose for posting it. As often as you can, take breaks from social media. Don't talk about it; be about it. We waste so much time on social media. The time we've spent tweeting could have been used to draw, write, workout, call a loved one, or focus on our goals. Take some time today to figure out how much time you are spending on social media. What is your time on social media hindering you from achieving? After some honest evaluation, take back the reigns on how you spend your time. Live in the moment of simplicity without unwarranted opinions and drama.

DAY SEVENTEEN

Dance Off

Harlem shake the hate, the doubt, the naysayers, and the negativity up off you. Straighten your crown and keep moving.

Besides the cabbage patch, the Harlem Shake is one of my favorite dances. It's just something about shaking things off you that don't serve you. It makes you feel good down to your core. Maybe the Harlem Shake isn't for you, but I dare you to take some time today to do your favorite dance. Turn your music up and turn everything else down. Have tons of fun doing it! Don't think about anything else besides feeling good physically, emotionally, and spiritually. You have many reasons to dance and carry a smile – not only today, but every day. Adding a happy dance to your routine is imperative. Negativity has no room to dance with you when you are dancing with yourself and all the blessings that are overflowing in your life. As you crank up your favorite tune, imagine me shouting, "Get it, sis! Get it, sis! Get it! Get it! I see you, girl!"

DAY EIGHTEEN

Think Future

Everything you are working hard for is not just for you but for your legacy. Build wisely, build with the future in mind.

We can sometimes be so selfish and build our lives with only us in mind. Sis, your legacy matters too. We must be careful not to think about the present moment without consideration of our future. If you have children or desire to have children, their future and the future of their children matters too. Don't be selfish in your pursuit of happiness and fulfilling your dreams. We must be mindful of what we put in the atmosphere as somethings have a hard time fading away. Building a legacy is more than just having money or businesses for your family to benefit from. Legacy is also about breaking curses and not allowing them to travel from generation to generation. We are all still learning, but as we learn, I pray that we act with our future in mind. Analyze every job, relationship, and opportunity. Before you say yes, or commit yourself to anything, consider how it will benefit or bring detriment to your future. Everyday, ask yourself, "What will I do today to change the narrative in my family? What curse will I break today? How am I going to make an investment that benefits my future?" How will this job help me in my future (even if you leave), is the relationship serving me and will it be beneficial to my future, am I doing something different that will break curses and change the narrative in my family? These are a few questions to consider when you are thinking about your legacy. Always remember that what you do today can and will impact your future.

DAY NINETEEN
In Control

You are in control of you. You are in control of your emotions. You do not have to respond to those in the same negative tone that you receive. You can respond in love or walk away. You are in control of you.

Would you believe me if I told you that there was a time in my life when I would fight anyone who even blinked at me wrong? What if I told you that I would chew you out really good if you came for me or mine? Or, that if you snapped at me, I would snap right back before you could finish snapping? I thank God for growth. I learned how to control my emotions and let things go. It isn't easy, but here are somethings I do to help me control my emotions:

- ♥ Meditation
- ♥ Stretching
- ♥ Praying
- ♥ Talking to friends who will talk you down & not make you want to turn up
- ♥ Walking/Exercising
- ♥ Crying when you are in a secluded area (crying is release.)
- ♥ Writing
- ♥ Completely walking away from the situation.

What helped me more than anything was realizing that my life is way more valuable and important than a clap back. Even though snapping at someone may be gratifying at the moment, it only makes you look immature later on. Sis, your life, purpose, gifts, and impact are too valuable for you to hand the reigns over to your emotions. Be intentional about managing your emotions and responses.

DAY TWENTY

say "NO"

Learning to say "Nah, I'm straight", will change
your life. It's okay to say no sis.

No is a complete sentence. You don't have to explain your decision to decline anything. There's more to life than partying. You are allowed to tell your friends that you don't feel like going. It's okay to not be in the mood to do any favors for anyone. If it's truly important, they will eventually get it done. It's okay to refuse to add tasks to your to-do list. You matter, Sis! If you keep doing everything for everybody or doing things that make everyone else happy, what will you do for you? "No" is powerful. "No" is a practice of self-care. Don't be mean about your, "no," but be firm and stick to it. If you are not in the mood, do not force it. Doing what makes you feel good matters. Now, before you go to work and tell your supervisor, *NO*, be smart and keep your job. However, just be mindful of saying yes to tasks that will drain you more than they serve you.

DAY TWENTY-ONE
Breathe

Listen, all you need is five minutes to focus on your breathing. Breathe in, breathe out. Take a moment, or as many as you need today, to just breathe.

One of the best things I decided to do was to give meditation a try. People may look at you sideways or think you are weird, but taking time to breathe and relax will change your life. We often think we need 15 to 30 minutes to meditate, but if five minutes is all you have, then five minutes is all you need. Use those five minutes to not stress or worry about anything. Use those five minutes to calm yourself and focus on the positivity that is happening around you. If you have high anxiety, meditation will be a useful tool for you. If you are unsure about it, do your research or find an accountability partner to try it with you. Try something different today. Meditate, sis!

"Breathe, stretch, shake, LET IT GO" —Mase

Am I the only one who LOVES Mase? I absolutely, positively, love Mase. Now, I don't love him more than God, but I will still turn the speakers up when a Mase song comes on. Breathe, stretch, shake is one of my favorite songs by him. It makes me want to get up, dance, and have fun, but it also reminds me that certain situations are totally out of my control and there is no point in stressing over them. Sometimes things will go exactly how we planned but sometimes things don't. The smallest and most unexpected situations will make us want to throw in the towel. We will invest so much energy into everything that went wrong that we fail to realize it's truly beyond our control. It is totally okay not to be in control. No matter what comes your way today, don't let it upset you, get you down, or get in the way of your plans. Take a deep breath, stretch, shake your shoulders loose, and let it go.

DAY TWENTY-THREE
Let Them Be

Everyone isn't going to do life the way that you do life. That's what makes them, THEM and you, YOU! Do what works best for you!

I absolutely dislike when we judge people because they don't operate like we do. Truthfully, I'm guilty of turning my nose up in the air when someone does something out of the norm. Sis, let's work on loving people for where they are and doing our best to understand why they do what they do. It may not make sense to us, but if it works for them, we shouldn't invest our energy into trying to change what they are doing. For example, maybe for your birthday, you like to have a big party. However, you have an associate who would rather relax on their birthday. While you may not agree with how they choose to celebrate their momentous occasion, you must respect their decision. After all, it's THEIR decision. If we took away the desire to be judgmental, we could learn a lot from each other. In your strive to be authentic, allow others the space to be themselves as well.

DAY TWENTY-FOUR

Conquer

Sometimes it's hard not to doubt yourself, but you've done hard before you can CONQUER this.

This is not the first time "hard" or its cousin "difficult" has knocked on your door and trust me when I say, it will not be the last. The Easy Read Version of the Bible for Romans 5:3-5 reads, "And we are also happy with the troubles we have. Why are we happy with troubles? Because we know that troubles make us more patient. And this patience is proof that we are strong. And this proof gives us hope. And this hope will never disappoint us. We know this because God has poured out his love to fill our hearts through the Holy Spirit he gave us." Yes, you read it right, we are happy with our troubles because troubles build our character and produces perseverance. If we can conquer one storm, we are able to conquer another. Sometimes, life will come in swinging and knock us off balance. These moments cause us to forget that we were already built to overcome trials and tribulations. Sis, I know you have hard days, but you are not new to hard. You handled it last time, so pick up your head, and handle it – again. You are a strong woman of God, right? So stand on His Word and walk in your victory!

DAY TWENTY-FIVE

Accept Defeat

This isn't the first time that you've come face to face with defeat and it most likely will not be the last.

One of my favorite writers is Maya Angelou and I quote her often! One of my favorite quotes by her is, *"You may encounter many defeats, but you must not be defeated. In fact, it may be necessary to encounter the defeats, so you can know who you are, what you can rise from, how you can still come out of it."*

What I learned from these words many years ago and what I constantly must remind myself is that defeat is a part of our process! Failure doesn't come so we can throw in the towel. Failure comes so that we can get up, dust ourselves off, and start over again! From failure, we learn what we are capable of. Take the moments of defeat to learn and form a new strategy. It's easy to give up, but it takes real hard work to walk into victories! You're a winner, Sis, so win!

DAY TWENTY-SIX

Inside Out

Listen sis, loving yourself goes deeper than the physical appearance. You got to learn to love your soul. Start from the inside out without conditions and watch how self-love will change your entire life.

Getting your hair and nails done will make you look pretty on the outside and possibly on the inside. However, if you are still broken to pieces internally, there is no amount of exterior upgrades that will make the brokenness go away. Yes, make yourself feel good by doing your hair, make-up, and buying a new outfit. Just don't forget to heal from past hurts, learn from mistakes, and get to the core of who you are. Learning and loving you takes work. It can be especially difficult when you deal with people or tasks that take more than they give. When you get to the core of loving yourself, everything that is important to the world will no longer be important to you. You will begin to make decisions based on what makes you feel good, not what others will think or say about it.

DAY TWENTY-SEVEN

Beg No One

Beg no one to stay in your life. If they want to leave give them room to do so.

top begging people to stay. Stop giving "one more chance" after "one more chance." If people can hurt you and walk away, let them leave. When people are for you and truly love you, you don't have to beg them to stay or treat you right. If they really wanted to be there, loving you, and treating you right would come natural. Even if they hurt you or make mistakes, they will put in the work to correct it and never do it again.

The saying, "People will only do to you what you allow," is true. You are not a revolving door. Stop allowing people to treat you as such. Can we be honest? Sometimes, we don't give people the space to leave. We become so attached to the fear that they won't return that we stay and deal with the unhealthiness. We lie about our happiness for the sake of keeping someone in our lives. When we are truly confident in what is ours, we can walk away with ease knowing that space isn't bad, but space is an opportunity to flourish. If you let it go and it doesn't come back, it wasn't meant to be, sis. That is okay because God never removes without replacing.

DAY TWENTY-EIGHT

Communicate

Communication is KEY. It is vital to learn appropriate ways to communicate your feelings. Don't sit on those feelings but don't yell, be rude, or disrespectful either.

Communication in all aspects of our lives is important. We must know how to communicate with friends, family, spouses, supervisors, co-workers, children, etc. A lack of communication can turn something small into something big – very quickly. If you are not understanding what is being voiced to you, instead of assuming, ask for clarification. Watch your tone and facial expressions because nonverbal communication matters. If someone was rude to you and you didn't like it, voice how you feel in a way that is to the point but respectful. If you are wrong, own up to it; pride can ruin great relationships. Communication is as only as hard as we make it.

If you truly desire to improve in this area, evaluate your communication skills. Ask other people to rate your communication on a scale of 1 to 5. Next, ask them for pointers on how you can improve your communication. Also, ask God to give you the strength and strategy you need to work on it. For this to be beneficial, you must remain open and not defensive. Take what others say and learn from it. This would make a great activity to do with your friends, family, and spouse. Remember, Sis, glowed up women communicate effectively.

DAY TWENTY-NINE

Superwoman

No one knows you need help if you do not ask. It is perfectly okay to ask for assistance. Put your pride or fear of being rejected to the side. No matter how big or how small it is. You never know who is willing to help if you don't ask.

We'll make a thousand excuses as to why we won't ask for help. We will allow past experiences to keep us from asking in the future. Some of us will even say that no one is willing to help without even asking. Asking for help can be hard, especially if we allow our pride to get in the way. Sis, asking for help doesn't take away your self-sufficiency. Instead, it eases the feeling of being overwhelmed and stressed out. Doing everything by yourself all the time is played out and doesn't make you superhuman. It makes you super tired, super burned out, and super mean. Seek some assistance today or this week, no matter how big or small the task is. Let people love on you by helping you.

DAY THIRTY
Fly High

Spread your wings and fly. There is a whole world out there waiting to see you.

The world is waiting for you to share your gifts, wisdom, and that beautiful energy that exudes from your soul. The world is longing to get to know who you are. Stop sitting on your greatness and act on it. The unknown is scary, I know, but you never know how far you will soar if you never leave the nest. If you want to move out the state or country, do it. If you want to make a bucket list of things to do before your next birthday, do it. If you want to write a book, do it. Whatever your heart desires, it is time to do it. There is no time like the present to step into your greatness. Give the world your magic, walk in your purpose, never stop creating, and do everything your heart desires. There is nothing off limits for you, Sis. God has got you covered. Work your faith and spread those wings. I am rooting for you and I can't wait to see what you have for the world!

DAY THIRTY-ONE

Finish Strong

Don't just start – FINISH!

To get to this point wasn't easy for me. This isn't the first book that I've written, but this is the first book that I have started, completed, and published. Most of us don't have a problem starting; we have a problem with being consistent and finishing. I pray that God replaces your urgency with patience. I pray that God increases your desire to finish and surrounds you with people who will be with you every step of the way – to the finish line and beyond. It's not about finishing first, it's about finishing in excellence! If you throw in the towel too soon, you will never see what the end will produce. Start strong, Sis, but finish stronger!

About the Author

Courtney Arlesia is your everyday woman with an extraordinary thirst for God. She prides herself on being a shining example of strength, empowerment, and inspiration to those around her. With a rugged start, Courtney has managed to obtain her Bachelor's degree in Social Work with a minor in Recording Industry, all while motivating and inspiring family, friends, and strangers with hopes that they too will fall in love with Christ. Courtney recently obtained her Masters of Science in Social Work in May of 2017, in an effort to expand her service in the community with the knowledge, experience, and research that she has gained throughout her educational career.

Being an aspiring writer, she is ferociously focused on writing inspiring blog posts and is beginning to gear more toward public speaking in an effort to expound upon her knowledge and research from her degrees and wisdom gained from life experiences.

Find out more about Courtney Arlesia, by visiting CourtneyArlesia.com

Acknowledgements

Writing and releasing my first book would never have happened without some amazing people. I am thankful for every person who has wished me nothing but success and has continuously encouraged me. I may not be able to list everyone's name but know if you have supported me since *Endless Love* days, attended events, shared events, took pictures, helped me create, allowed me to speak at your events, or even mentioned my name to anybody with positive things to follow this thank you is for you as well.

To my Parents, Timmie and Metoyer Clardy, who would have thought I'd be where I am in life, receiving my Master's and now an author? Everything I am is because you two saw fit to take a chance on love at a very young age. I pray that through my accomplishments God continues to strengthen your marriage. I know I haven't been the perfect daughter but you created me and here we are. Every time I win, you two win! Nothing can stop that. Thank you for loving me, being patient with me, and never pushing me away despite any mistakes I made.

To my brother, Corey, and his five beautiful children. You are a cool big brother. You are blessed and your blessings have blessed me. I pray that me chasing my dreams will forever encourage you to chase yours. There is nothing off limits for you. I love you forever and always.

To my cousin and the designer of my book cover, Lyric Abbott of Visionary Palette. I should have known you were full of talent, we are products of Taylors which means we got the juice. I am beyond proud of you. I cannot thank you enough for your amazing time, talent, and patience it took to produce this cover. You go, girl! Never stop being great.

To my very dear close friends, whom I consider to be sisters and brothers to me, I cannot thank you enough. The ones that have prayed with me, cried with me, supported me, seen me at my lowest and still pushed me to highest. The ones that showed up to events, bought T-Shirts, and who will be screaming to the rooftops about this book. I do not have to mention your names because you know who you are and I love each one of you. I'm so grateful for the things we have accomplished in our lives. In the words of Drake: me and all my [people] doing well, doing well dog.

To my sweet angel, Caleb Anthony Slater. I will never forget the day I found out I was pregnant and I will never forget the moment I loss you. I often wonder what my life would be like if you were still here but even in your absence you have taught me so much. You pushed me to grow up. At 23 I thought I had it all figured out but you showed me otherwise. Here I am at 27 and four years later and I'll be forever grateful for you. Thank you coming into my world and waking me up. It's an amazing feeling knowing all that I can do just because of you. I love you always.

Lastly but most importantly, to my Lord and Savior Jesus Christ. The one who gave me this gift, the one who covers me, keeps me, protects me, and LOVES me without conditions. I ran from You but You waited on me and welcomed me with open arms. Don't get me wrong because I still make mistakes and even up to this day, I took some detours and made mistakes but I am so thankful that You are a forgiving and understanding God. I can only hope I am making You proud. I pray that when someone purchases this book and reads it that they don't see me but they see what You have done and what You are doing in my life. You an awesome wonder and Your praise will forever flow from my lips. I love you so much God and no one can take me away from You!

Stay Connected

Thank you for purchasing, Glow Up, Sis, Glow Up! Courtney would like to connect with you. Below are a few ways you can stay posted on new releases, speaking engagements, events, and more. Courtney can't wait to meet you!

INSTAGRAM Courtney.Arlesia

FACEBOOK Endless Love Group

WEBSITE www.CourtneyArlesia.Com

EMAIL Courtney@CourtneyArlesia.com